I0876837

USC TROJANS

BY

ALEXANDER LOWE

INSIDE COLLEGE FOOTBALL

MEDIA ENHANCED BOOKS AV² BY WEIGL ADDED VALUE • AUDIO VISUAL

www.av2books.com

AV² provides enriched content that supplements and complements this book. Weigl's AV² books strive to create inspired learning and engage young minds in a total learning experience.

Go to www.av2books.com, and enter this book's unique code.

BOOK CODE

AVZ93249

AV² by Weigl brings you media enhanced books that support active learning.

Your AV² Media Enhanced books come alive with...

Audio Listen to sections of the book read aloud.

Video Watch informative video clips.

Embedded Weblinks Gain additional information for research.

Try This! Complete activities and hands-on experiments.

Key Words Study vocabulary, and complete a matching word activity.

Quizzes Test your knowledge.

Slideshow View images and captions, and prepare a presentation.

... and much, much more!

Published by AV² by Weigl
350 5th Avenue, 59th Floor
New York, NY 10118
Website: www.av2books.com

Library of Congress Control Number: 2018968223

ISBN 978-1-7911-0138-1 (hardcover)
ISBN 978-1-7911-0139-8 (multi-user eBook)
ISBN 978-1-7911-0140-4 (single-user eBook)

Printed in Guangzhou, China
1 2 3 4 5 6 7 8 9 0 23 22 21 20 19

042019
102318

Project Coordinator: Jared Siemens Designer: Terry Paulhus

Every reasonable effort has been made to trace ownership and to obtain permission to reprint copyright material. The publishers would be pleased to have any errors or omissions brought to their attention so that they may be corrected in subsequent printings.

The publisher acknowledges Alamy, Getty Images, and Wikimedia Commons as its primary image suppliers for this title.

INSIDE COLLEGE FOOTBALL

USC Trojans

CONTENTS

Introduction

The University of Southern California (USC) Trojans are one of the most successful teams in all of college football. The team has more than 800 wins since it first took the field, including seven National Championships. The team's 80 **All-Americans** and six **Heisman Memorial Trophy** winners show a level of success that few programs can match.

The sight of a Trojan can strike fear into the hearts of opposing fans across the nation. That intimidation can appear in the form of a Trojan on the back of Traveler the horse, or the USC drum major stabbing a sword into the turf before the game. USC's famous fight song "Fight On!" is one of the most recognizable in all of sports. The Trojan marching band plays it after every first down, haunting the opponents' defense, who gave up yet another big play to the boys in cardinal and gold.

Cornerback Ajene Harris recorded 89 tackles in 41 career games with the Trojans. He also scored three touchdowns on defensive interceptions.

Historic Programs such as USC are known for their **rivalries**. Some of the USC's best-known rivalries are with the University of California, Los Angeles (UCLA), the University of Notre Dame, and Stanford University. Beyond these **matchups**, there is no shortage of other games on the schedule to get the fans fired up to cheer on the Trojans.

Velus Jones Jr. led the Trojans in kick returns, with 21 returns for 483 yards in the 2018 season. Jones ranks 12th on USC's career kickoff return list.

USC

Stadium Los Angeles Memorial Coliseum

Division Pacific-12 (Pac-12) South

Head Coach Clay Helton

Location Los Angeles, California

National Championships 7

Nicknames USC, Trojans

6 Heisman Memorial Trophy Winners

81 First-Round NFL Draft Picks

12 Pro Football Hall of Famers

44 College Football Hall of Fame Inductees

History

In **1946**, Trojan marching band member and place-kicker **Tommy Walker** wrote the fanfare song "The Charge," now heard at stadiums across the nation.

Coach John McKay's 1972 Trojans are considered one of the greatest teams in the history of college football. The Trojans were the first team ever to be named number one on both the coaches' and media polls.

The first USC Trojans team took the field in 1888. Before the team was known as the Trojans, it was referred to as the Methodists. This was because the Methodist Church helped run the school. The team officially became the Trojans in 1912.

Since the 1920s, the Trojans have been an overwhelmingly successful team. One of the best eras was from 1928 to 1933, when the team won two National Championships under Coach Howard Jones. Another impressive period was when Coach John McKay led the team to three National Championships in the 1960s and early 1970s. The team also had three Heisman winners over those two decades, an impressive amount for any single school. In 1972, the Trojans had a perfect 12–0 season and crushed the Ohio State University Buckeyes in the Rose Bowl.

The modern era has seen great success for USC as well. In 2009, the team was named team of the decade by multiple sports news outlets. For most of that decade, the Trojans were coached by Pete Carroll. USC was ranked fourth or higher in national rankings during 7 of Carroll's 10 seasons as coach. USC is a consistent bowl threat and an intimidating matchup for nearly every opponent.

USC's first opponent was the Alliance Athletic Club (AAC). USC played the AAC twice during the 1888–89 season and won both games. In 1889, the Trojans played their first college opponent, St. Vincent's College, which later became Loyola Marymount University.

The Stadium

The Los Angeles Coliseum has been home to 22 athletic teams and has hosted many local, national, and international sporting events. The Coliseum has also served as a set for multiple films, television shows, and advertisements.

The Trojans play in the Los Angeles Memorial Coliseum, a giant stadium in Los Angeles. The Coliseum is not just the home of the Trojans, though they have played there since the first year it was open. Many other events are also hosted there. It was originally built as a memorial to LA veterans of World War I (1914–1918). The Coliseum serves as the home of the Los Angeles Rams. The Raiders also played there when they were located in Los Angeles. It was one of the main sites of the Olympics in 1932 and 1984. The Olympics will be hosted there again in 2028.

The Coliseum is the largest stadium in both the Pac-12 Conference and the National Football League (NFL). Before 2018, the stadium had a seating capacity of 94,000. The most recent updates decreased the seating by about 16,000 seats, but added modern lighting and technology, including Wi-Fi and new scoreboards.

One of the Coliseum's unique traditions is USC's Song Girls. This dance team takes the place of traditional cheerleaders. They have worn the same iconic uniforms since their debut in 1967. During each halftime show, the Song Girls perform a dance routine with the Trojan Marching Band, which is also known as "The Spirit of Troy."

The Spirit of Troy has two platinum records and has performed with numerous musical acts, including Beyoncé and Radiohead. The band has also performed at the Academy Awards and the Grammy Awards.

Where They Play

Welcome to the Los Angeles Coliseum, home of the University of Southern California Trojans. The Coliseum is one of Southern California's best-known landmarks. Known for hosting many important gatherings and sporting events, the Coliseum is filled with rich history. The Trojans have been winning games there since 1923, and fans continue to flock to the Coliseum for USC football every fall.

PAC-12 NORTH

1. **Oregon State University**
   Corvallis, Oregon
2. **Stanford University**
   Stanford, California
3. **University of California**
   Berkeley, California
4. **University of Oregon**
   Eugene, Oregon
5. **University of Washington**
   Seattle, Washington
6. **Washington State University**
   Pullman, Washington

Arena
Los Angeles Memorial Coliseum

Location
Los Angeles, California

Broke Ground
December 21, 1921

Completed
May 1, 1923

Surface
Real Grass

Features
- The Olympic Cauldron is lit during USC football games
- Memorial Court of Honor plaques honor people important to the Coliseum
- A record 104,953 attended a game in 1947

PAC-12 SOUTH

1. **Arizona State University**
   Tempe, Arizona
2. **University of Arizona**
   Tucson, Arizona
3. **University of California, Los Angeles**
   Los Angeles, California
4. **University of Colorado**
   Boulder, Colorado
5. ★ **University of Southern California**
   Los Angeles, California
6. **University of Utah**
   Salt Lake City, Utah

WASHINGTON
OREGON
IDAHO
MONTANA
NORTH DAKOTA
SOUTH DAKOTA
MINNESOTA
WISCONSIN
WYOMING
IOWA
NEBRASKA
NEVADA
UTAH
COLORADO
KANSAS
MISSOURI
CALIFORNIA
ARIZONA
NEW MEXICO
OKLAHOMA
ARKANSAS
TEXAS
LOUISIANA
Pacific Ocean
1
2
3
4
5
6
SCALE
0 miles
500 miles
0 kilometers
500 km
LEGEND
Home Stadium
Pac-12 North
Pac-12 South
United States
Other Countries
Water

The Uniforms

The **first** football helmet was made of **moleskin** and was worn in 1893 by **Admiral Joseph Reeves**, who played football for the U.S. Naval Academy.

- The Trojans and their fans value tradition, and as a result, only minor tweaks have been made to USC's uniforms over the years. In fact, the current Trojans uniform has looked almost exactly the same since 2002.

The Trojans' uniform colors are gold and cardinal. Cardinal is a deep shade of red. Their uniforms have always reflected these colors in some way. The current uniform features cardinal jerseys at home and white on the road. Both uniforms have gold pants.

The team first wore hard shell helmets in 1950. Those first helmets were cardinal with a gold stripe down the middle. Five years later, a diamond was added on the side, but that only lasted for one year. In 1972, a Trojan **logo** was placed on the helmet. Some version of the Trojan has appeared on the helmets ever since.

Another hallmark of the USC uniforms is that there are no names on the jerseys. The Trojans are the only team to have never featured the players' names on the back. Even schools that traditionally do not feature names have included them for special uniforms, but USC has held firm in this tradition.

Before the Trojan head became a permanent fixture on USC's helmets, the team's helmets had player numbers on the side or were left completely blank. With the exception of gold helmets during the 1957 season, the Trojans have always worn a cardinal red helmet.

Student Athletes

Actor **John Wayne**, famous for his nearly 80 Western **films**, played football at USC.

Olaijah Griffin, son of rapper and hip-hop producer Warren G, debuted as a cornerback for the Trojans in a game versus the University of Nevada, Las Vegas (UNLV) Rebels, where he logged three solo tackles.

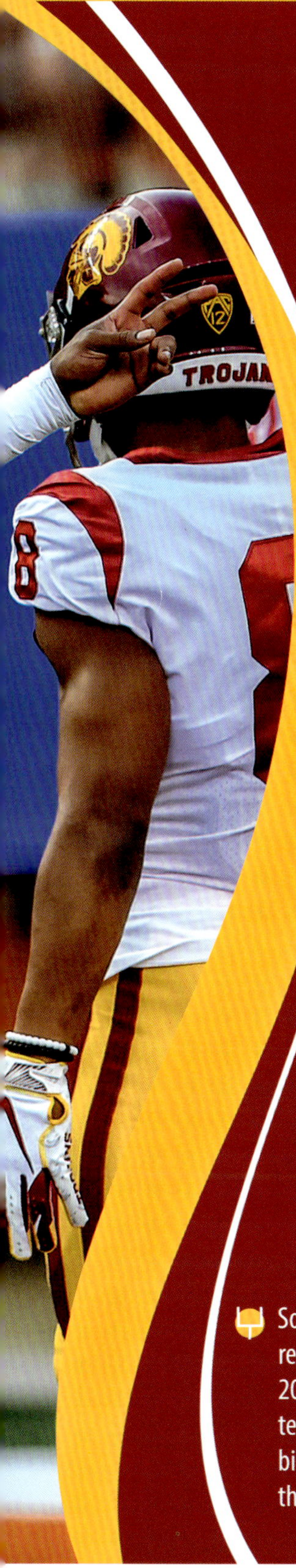

Being a college student athlete is hard work. Student athletes have to perform well on the football field and in the classroom. USC student athletes are required to meet a minimum grade point average and attend all of their classes. They must also have 12 academic credits per term. USC has an extensive Student-Athlete Academic Services Program. It is designed to help student athletes reach their full potential academically, personally, and professionally.

Many student athletes are given athletic scholarships. An athletic scholarship is a financial aid agreement between the athlete and the college or university. Athletes who do not receive an athletic scholarship can be "walk-on" members of the team. This means they are on the team, but without athletic financial aid. USC typically awards the maximum number of football scholarships allowed, which is 85.

Sophomore Erik Krommenhoek received honorable mention for the 2018 Pac-12 All-Academic football team. Krommenhoek, a human biology major, maintained a 3.11 GPA throughout the 2018 season.

Bowl Games

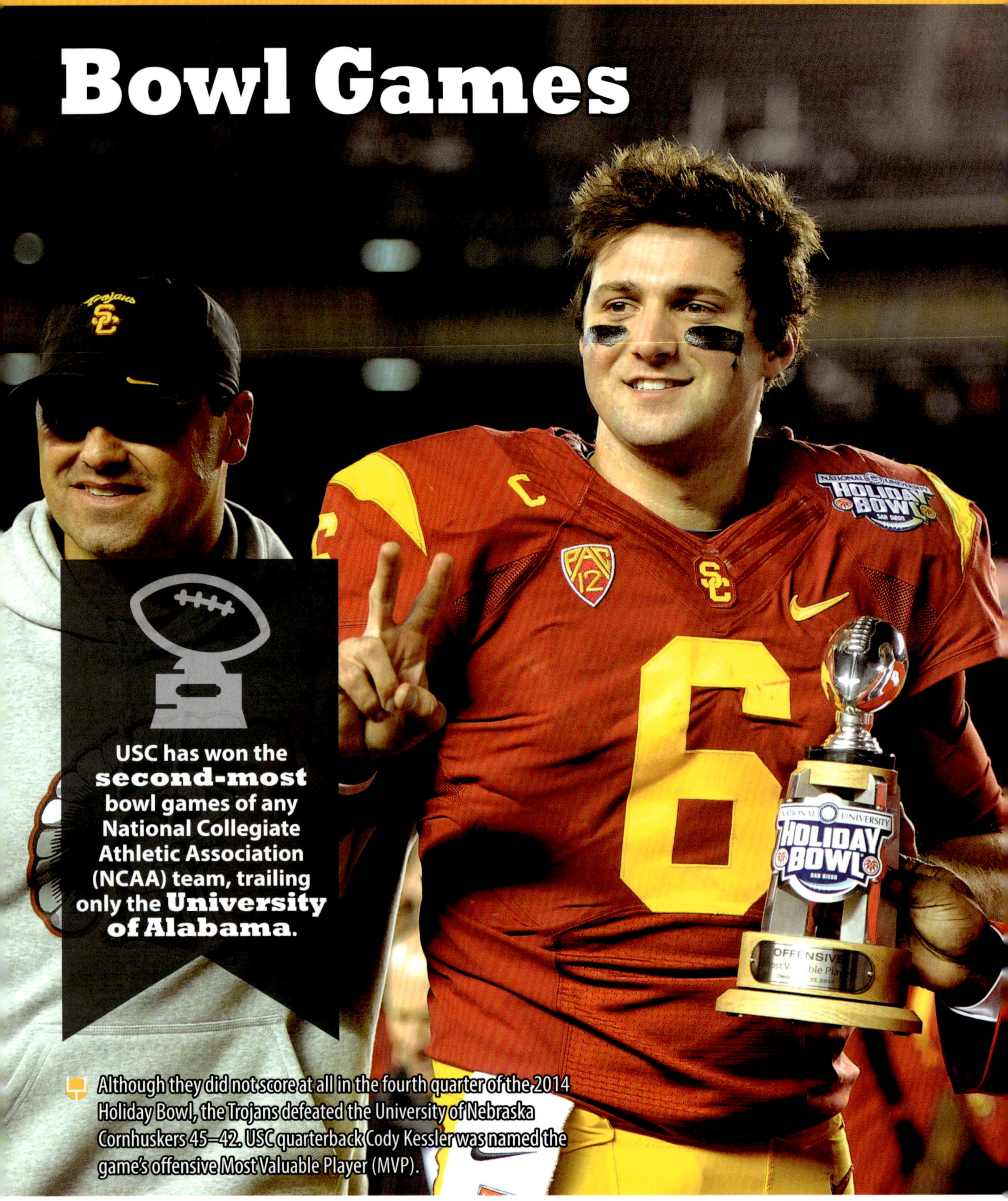

USC has won the **second-most** bowl games of any National Collegiate Athletic Association (NCAA) team, trailing only the **University of Alabama**.

Although they did not score at all in the fourth quarter of the 2014 Holiday Bowl, the Trojans defeated the University of Nebraska Cornhuskers 45–42. USC quarterback Cody Kessler was named the game's offensive Most Valuable Player (MVP).

Bowl games are a unique sports tradition in college football. In the beginning of college football, there was no true **postseason**. Today, a variety of postseason bowl games are played. Bowl games give teams the opportunity to continue striving for recognition and victory after the end of regular play. There are currently 40 bowl games played in various combinations each year. These games are chosen with input from teams, sponsors, and the College Football Playoff Selection Committee. The game matchups are announced in December.

The most notable bowl for the Trojans is the Rose Bowl. The team has appeared in 34 Rose Bowls and has won 25, both of which are Rose Bowl records. The Trojans have won 64.9 percent of their bowl games, the highest bowl game winning percentage of teams with at least 25 bowl appearances.

Ronald Jones II played as a running back for the Trojans from 2015 to 2017. He played in a bowl game each season, including the Trojans' 52–49 Rose Bowl win against Pennsylvania State University in 2017.

The Coaches

In 1951, **Howard Jones** was elected to the **first-ever** class of the College Football Hall of Fame.

Clay Helton started as the quarterbacks coach at USC in 2010 and then served as interim head coach twice before being named the team's head coach at the end of the 2015 season.

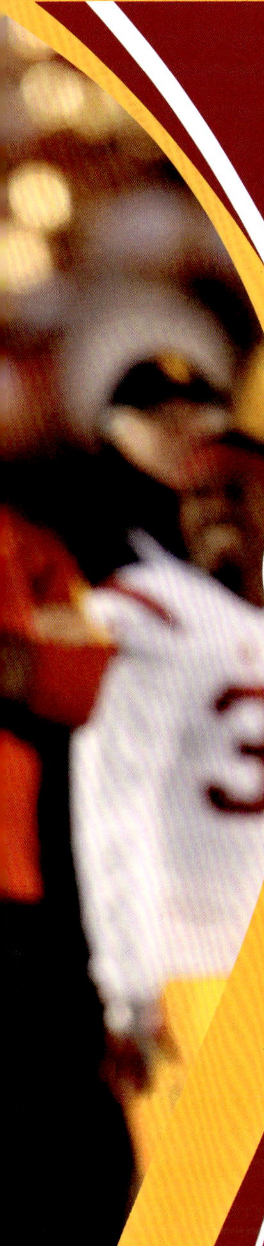

The USC Trojans have had 23 coaches since Henry H. Goddard first led the team in 1888. Some of football's best coaching minds have stood on the sidelines of the Coliseum. Many assistants have gone on to become head coaches of other schools. Multiple coaches have also worked in the NFL after their time at USC.

HOWARD JONES Howard Jones is regarded by many as the best coach in college football history. His most notable years were at USC, where he coached from 1925 to 1940. He led the Trojans to seven conference championships, two National Championships, and five Rose Bowl victories over his 16 seasons. He also coached the team to a 76–0 victory in the Trojans' first-ever matchup with rival UCLA.

PETE CARROLL In recent Trojan history, Pete Carroll is one of the most beloved coaches to pace the Coliseum's sideline. He was at USC from 2001 until 2009 and led the team to a 34-game winning streak from 2003 to 2005. He is one of only three coaches in history to win both an NCAA National Championship and a **Super Bowl** during his coaching career. Carroll coached the Seattle Seahawks to their Super Bowl win in 2014.

CLAY HELTON Clay Helton is the current head coach of USC. After a playing career at Auburn University and the University of Houston, he began coaching. He was originally hired at USC as the quarterback coach in 2010. In 2015, he became the team's head coach. He led USC to a bowl game in each of his first three years with the Trojans, and the team has finished with a winning record in three of his four seasons.

The Mascot

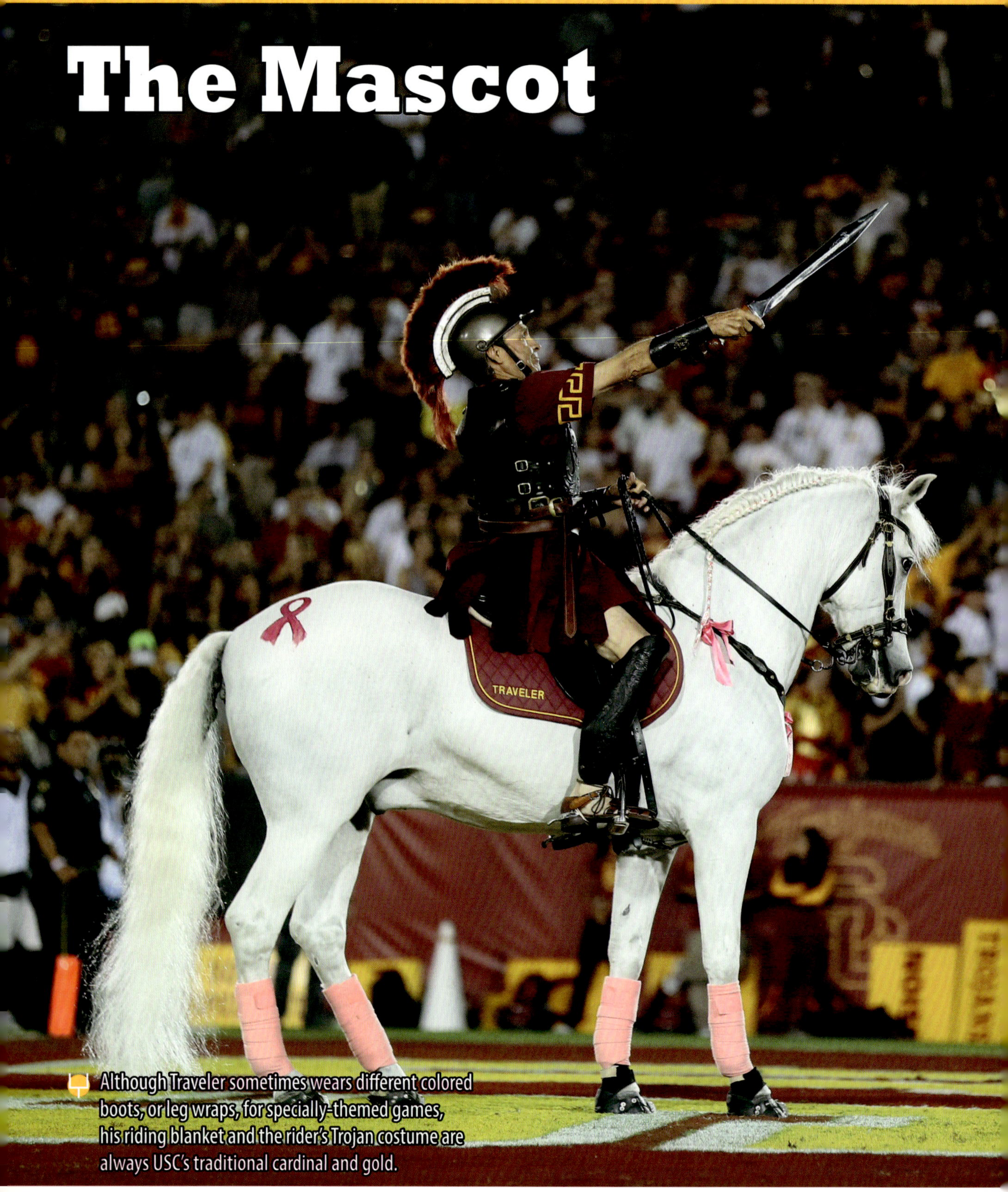

Although Traveler sometimes wears different colored boots, or leg wraps, for specially-themed games, his riding blanket and the rider's Trojan costume are always USC's traditional cardinal and gold.

The Trojan mascot is unique in college sports. USC's official on-field mascot is a live horse. The horse's name is Traveler. At games, a costumed Trojan rides Traveler. The Trojans were a famous group of ancient warriors known for their smart and fierce battle techniques, and USC takes its team name from them.

Traveler first appeared at a game in 1961. Previously, the stadium had a track around the field, and Traveler would run a lap after each Trojan score. Now, following every touchdown, Traveler runs along the sideline to the approval of thousands of cheering fans. The current Traveler is named Traveler IX. He started appearing at USC games in 2017.

The original Traveler, who was introduced in 1961, was ridden by his owner, Richard Saukko, a local horse trainer. Saukko served as the official rider until 1988. Since then, riders have all been USC alumni.

Legends of the Past

For many players, their time with the Trojans is the start of a promising football career. These are some of the best-known football players to play for the University of Southern California.

Marcus Allen

Marcus Allen was **recruited** to USC as a defensive back, but he moved to tailback during his freshman year. That move proved to be a smart one. He went on to have 11 200-yard rushing games, which is a tie for the NCAA record. Allen also won the Heisman in 1981 and was **drafted** 10th overall the following year by the Los Angeles Raiders. USC has since retired his number 33 jersey. He also won the Maxwell Player of the Year Award and the Walter Camp Award, both given to the top player in college football. Allen retired from the NFL in 1997.

Position: Running Back
Seasons: 1978–1981 (USC Trojans), 1982–1992 (Los Angeles Raiders), 1993–1997 (Kansas City Chiefs)
Born: March 26, 1960, San Diego, California

Carson Palmer

Carson Palmer had a collegiate career that marks him as one of the best quarterbacks of all time. He took over as the USC starter for his sophomore season and was successful from the start. Under Coach Pete Carroll's high-powered offense, Palmer put up outstanding statistics, including 33 touchdown passes, and was rewarded with the Heisman Trophy in 2002. He ended his USC career as the Pacific-10 (Pac-10) career leader for completions, attempts, and passing yards. He was then drafted first overall by the Cincinnati Bengals. Palmer retired from the NFL after the 2017 season.

Position: Quarterback
Seasons: 1998–2002 (USC Trojans), 2003–2010 (Cincinatti Bengals), 2011–2012 (Oakland Raiders), 2013–2017 (Arizona Cardinals)
Born: December 27, 1979, Fresno, California

Ronnie Lott

Before Ronnie Lott was drafted eighth overall in the 1981 NFL draft, he was a team captain for the USC Trojans. As a part of a tough defense that only gave up 11.8 points per game, Lott helped lead the team to a 1978 National Championship and Rose Bowl appearances in 1979 and 1980. In 1980, Lott was named an All-American after intercepting eight passes. After 14 successful seasons in the NFL, he retired before the 1995 season. He was later inducted into the USC Athletic Hall of Fame, and in 2002 he was inducted into the College Football Hall of Fame.

Position: Defensive Back
Seasons: 1977–1980 (USC Trojans), 1981–1990 (San Francisco 49ers), 1991–1992 (Los Angeles Raiders), 1993–1994 (New York Jets)
Born: May 8, 1959, Albuquerque, New Mexico

Keyshawn Johnson

One of the most entertaining wide receivers in NFL history, Keyshawn Johnson made his name at USC. While there, he was a two-time All-American. He was also the 1995 Cotton Bowl MVP. Johnson only played in one Rose Bowl, but his 216 receiving yards and one touchdown was impressive enough to get him inducted into the Rose Bowl Hall of Fame in 2008. USC fans can still hear from Johnson, who currently works part-time as an analyst on ESPN Los Angeles radio.

Position: Wide Receiver
Seasons: 1992–1993 (West Los Angeles College Wildcats), 1994–1995 (USC Trojans), 1996–1999 (New York Jets), 2000–2003 (Tampa Bay Buccaneers), 2004–2005 (Dallas Cowboys), 2006 (Carolina Panthers)
Born: July 22, 1972, Los Angeles, California

All-Time Records

12,327

Career Passing Yards

Matt Barkley threw for the most yards of any USC quarterback, with a total of 12,327 passing yards in his career.

345

Single-Game Receiving Yards

Marqise Lee gained 345 receiving yards in a 2012 game against the University of Arizona, making him the USC single-game leader.

35.1
Average Kickoff Return Yards
Anthony Davis holds the NCAA record for average yards per kickoff return, with 35.1.

92.9
Percent of Field Goals Made
Mario Danelo made 92.9 percent of his field goals, which is a USC record.

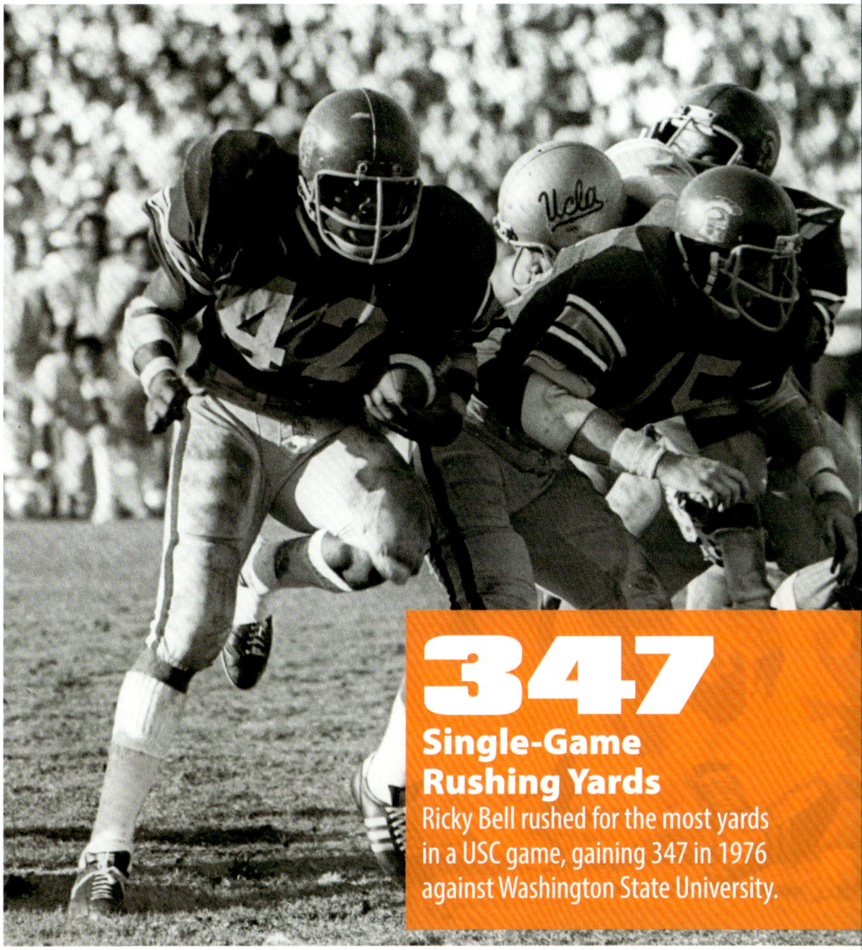

347
Single-Game Rushing Yards
Ricky Bell rushed for the most yards in a USC game, gaining 347 in 1976 against Washington State University.

Timeline

Throughout the team's history, the USC Trojans have had many memorable events that have become defining moments for the team and its fans.

1888
The first USC football team takes the field.

1900

In 1912, the team changes its name to the Trojans.

1920

1923
The Trojans win their first Rose Bowl, defeating the Penn State University Nittany Lions 14–3.

1931
The Trojans win their first national title.

1940

1951
Coach Howard Jones is inducted into the College Football Hall of Fame.

1960

1965
Running back Mike Garrett wins the first Trojan Heisman Trophy.

The Future

Under the current coaching staff, USC has seen success at the conference and national levels. With the program's strong sense of tradition and pride, there will be no shortage of talented recruits who want to come to Los Angeles and wear the cardinal and gold of the Trojans. The future looks very bright for Trojans fans.

1977
Frank Gifford is elected to the Pro Football Hall of Fame, the first Trojan player to be inducted.

2002–2008
USC wins seven-straight conference championships, a program best.

In 2017, the Trojans win the Pac-12, the 39th conference title in school history.

1980 — 2000 — 2020

2002
Carson Palmer wins the Heisman Trophy, becoming the first USC quarterback to win the award.

2016
Coach Clay Helton takes over for his first full season as head coach.

Write a Biography

Life Story

A person's life story can be the subject of a book. This kind of book is called a biography. Biographies often describe the lives of people who have achieved great success. These people may be alive today, or they may have lived many years ago. Reading a biography can help you learn more about a great person.

Get the Facts

Use this book, and research in the library and on the internet, to find out more about your favorite player. Learn as much about him as you can. What position does he play? What are his statistics in important categories? Has he set any records? Also, be sure to write down key events in the person's life. What was his childhood like? What has he accomplished off the field? Is there anything else that makes this person special or unusual?

Use the Concept Web

A concept web is a useful research tool. Read the questions in the concept web on the following page. Answer the questions in your notebook. Your answers will help you write a biography.

Concept Web

Write a Biography

Adulthood

- Where does this individual currently reside?
- Does he have a family?

Your Opinion

- What did you learn from the books you read in your research?
- Would you suggest these books to others?
- Was anything missing from these books?

Childhood

- Where and when was this person born?
- Describe his parents, siblings, and friends.
- Did he grow up in unusual circumstances?

Accomplishments off the Field

- What is this person's life's work?
- Has he received awards or recognition for accomplishments?
- How have this person's accomplishments served others?

Help and Obstacles

- Did this individual have a positive attitude?
- Did he receive help from others?
- Did this person have a mentor?
- Did this person face any hardships?
- If so, how were the hardships overcome?

Accomplishments on the Field

- What records does this person hold?
- What key games and plays have defined his career?
- What are his stats in categories important to his position?

Work and Preparation

- What was this person's education?
- What was his work experience?
- How does this person work?
- What is the process he uses?

Trivia Time

Take this quiz to test your knowledge of the USC Trojans. The answers are printed upside down under each question.

1 Which quarterback was drafted first overall by the Cincinnati Bengals in 2003?

A. Carson Palmer

2 What is the name of the USC fight song?

A. "Fight On!"

3 Which position did Clay Helton coach for USC before becoming head coach?

A. Quarterback

4 Who holds the USC career passing yards record?

A. Matt Barkley

5 Where do the Trojans play their home games?

A. The Los Angeles Memorial Coliseum

6 When will the Olympics be held in Los Angeles again?

A. 2028

7 Which NFL team did Pete Carroll coach to a Super Bowl?

A. The Seattle Seahawks

8 In what year did the first USC football team play?

A. 1888

9 What position did Keyshawn Johnson play?

A. Wide receiver

10 Which coach led USC to five Rose Bowl victories?

A. Howard Jones

Key Words

All-Americans: a player, usually in high school or college, judged to be the best in each position of a sport

drafted: chosen by the National Football League to play professionally for a specific team

Heisman Memorial Trophy: an annual award given to the college football player who best demonstrates excellence and hard work

logo: a symbol that stands for a team or organization

matchups: contests between two athletes or sports teams

postseason: a sporting event that takes place after the end of the regular season

recruited: to be asked to enroll as a member of an organization

rivalries: competitions between different groups or individuals toward the same objective or goal

Super Bowl: the NFL's annual championship game between the winning team from the National Football Conference and the winning team from the American Football Conference

Index

Log on to www.av2books.com

AV^2 by Weigl brings you media enhanced books that support active learning. Go to www.av2books.com, and enter the special code found on page 2 of this book. You will gain access to enriched and enhanced content that supplements and complements this book. Content includes video, audio, weblinks, quizzes, a slideshow, and activities.

AV^2 Online Navigation

Audio
Listen to sections of the book read aloud.

Book Pages
AV^2 pages directly correspond to pages in the book.

Video
Watch informative video clips.

Embedded Weblinks
Gain additional information for research.

Key Words
Study vocabulary, and complete a matching word activity.

Try This!
Complete activities and hands-on experiments.

Quizzes
Test your knowledge.

Slideshow
View images and captions, and prepare a presentation.

AV^2 was built to bridge the gap between print and digital. We encourage you to tell us what you like and what you want to see in the future.

Sign up to be an AV^2 Ambassador at www.av2books.com/ambassador.

Due to the dynamic nature of the internet, some of the URLs and activities provided as part of AV^2 by Weigl may have changed or ceased to exist. AV^2 by Weigl accepts no responsibility for any such changes. All media enhanced books are regularly monitored to update addresses and sites in a timely manner. Contact AV^2 by Weigl at 1-866-649-3445 or av2books@weigl.com with any questions, comments, or feedback.